"I hated this book. It is in the worst possible taste. I don't want my name in any way associated with something so repugnant."

Sidney Sheldon

FINAL EXIT FOR CATS

A FELINE SUICIDE GUIDE

BY MICHAEL VINER
ILLUSTRATED BY FRANK REMKIEWICZ

HarperCollins*Publishers*

HarperCollins books may be purchased for educational, business, or sales promotional use. For information, please write: Special Markets Department, HarperCollins Publishers, Inc., 10 East 53rd Street, New York, NY 10022.

FIRST EDITION

Designed by: Claudyne Bianco

LIBRARY OF CONGRESS CATALOG CARD NUMBER 92-52681

ISBN 0-06-096961-X

92 93 94 95 96 CW 10 9 8 7 6 5 4 3 2 1

Part I

WHY FINAL EXIT?
INTOLERABLE situations,
that's why. Like when
they bring home a
Rottweiler puppy...

...or a new kitten...

... or when the town passes a leash law for cats...

... or when they keep buying huge bags of that dried stuff even though your teeth are not what they used to be... or even <u>where</u> they used to be...

... or the new baby is getting all the attention, even though you try to show your acceptance by climbing into the crib to sleep... on his head.

You'll get ideas. Even that light bulb in the balloon over your head can help if you unscrew it and stick your paw in the socket. Read on for more exciting Final Exits.

Part II
In The Kitchen

Some of the best parties
end up in the kitchen.
So can your best Final Exit.
Here's how...

The microwave.
Write a note. Put
the casserole pot
in the oven, climb
in. Wait.

Find the blender.
Plug it in. Now put it
on like a hat. Use a
long spoon to push the
button marked 'puree!

The best-smelling way to go. Put half the ingredients in the bread maker. Push the buttons for quick sourdough loaf. Climb in. Wait.

Get your tail and one leg way down in the garbage disposal. Now stretch... turn the switch on.

Thanksgiving morning is a good time for a Final Exit. You'll find the turkey in the fridge. If it's stuffed, and if it's oyster stuffing, eat all of it. Then climb into the cavity. Pull the door shut. Pull the turkey shut... Wait.

The trash compactor.
Pull it out. Hide
under the trash.
Bring something
for covering yourself...
like the sports
page.

The freezer. Find the wrapping paper and the tape. Wrap and tape yourself. Save your head and one paw for last. Notice the writing on the packages... GROUND SIRLOIN, CHICKEN BREASTS, ETC. Write SURPRISE! ON your wrapping... Wait.

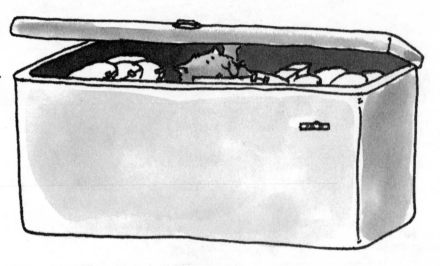

The electric can opener.
Since dry cat food came along
you don't hear it's wonderful
sound much anymore. Shove
a pawful of neckskin into
it. Get ready to spin around.

Dress up like Dracula.
Find a chopstick and shove
it into the pencil sharpener.
Hold it against your chest.
Fall forward. This will
really confuse them.

Part III
Around The House

Most Final Exits happen in the home. The lounge singer method. Jump into the piano. Lean on the stick. Sing.

Sometimes it's just a matter of waiting.

Your favorite windowsill.
How they marvel when you
run and jump up there...
Six stories from the
pavement! Smear it
with Vaseline.

The cooling fan. Nice to sit in front of, but a cool Final Exit if you remove that screen... and get really close.

The Hot Tub. Find the bottle of Chardonnay, the big one. Drink it all. Wrap a towel around your neck. Fill the bottle from the tub. Hang on to it. Jump in.

Dial that number that makes your own phone ring. When they leave the lawnmower to answer it, crawl way, way under the mower. Wait.

If you thrill to the speed and precision of a fine motorcar, try this one: Open the hood. Drink all the brake fluid. Close the hood. Sit in the car and beg to go for a ride.

Set the dryer for one hour...on high. Get in. Take along some of those good-smelling odorizers. No clothes. Do this when there's no one around to hear the thumps.

Start the car.
Wear the shower cap.
Attach the vacuum
cleaner hose to the
exhaust pipe. Shove
it under the cap.
Wait.

Get the fireplace roaring and cozy. Climb up on the roof. Wedge yourself into the chimney. Wear a Santa hat.

Pitch yourself head first from their highest stairway. Keep your neck stiff. Leave a banana peel on the top step. Maybe they'll find it later.

Move the magnifying glass so it makes a tiny dot of light on the oriental rug... the good one. Go to sleep on the dot.

You don't have to be
in Texas for this one.
Sneak into that stack
of wood in the sawbuck.
Get real stiff. Not
much waiting involved.

Smother yourself in a great Final Exit. Chew a whole pack of bubble gum. Smear it all over your face. Get in the car... the new one with the air bag. Release the brake. Roll into the neighbor's new wagon.

Ever want to be on TV? Look at the VCR. Find the buttons marked Power and Fast Forward. Did you know that your head can fit in that slot? Well, it can. Squeeze hard. Push both buttons.

Take an enemy with
you if you can.

The old light socket
trick. Be sure to lick
your paw first. Not
that one, the other
one!

Move the garden spade to the very end of the nail. Lay down and kick the wall as hard as you can. Do this during Spring bulb planting time.

Lift up that thing behind the toilet. See the brick? Dive down there and hug the brick. Don't let go. Do this during a dinner party.

Wait til they're out with the car. Loop your flea collar around the door latch inside the garage. When they return they'll press the button for the electric garage door opener. Be patient.

Smell that chicken? It's all for you. Open the lid of the Bar-B-Q. Eat every piece. Now hop in and close the lid. A potholder helps.

The gasoline is in the garage near the mower. Find a small bucket. Empty the bird bath. Fill it with gasoline. Some bird seed on the bucket is a nice touch. Have matches ready.

Near the pool you'll find the skimmer. Also the portable stereo. Place the skimmer near the pool. Shove the boom box into it. Crawl in with it. Roll over.

Wait till they buy two bags of Kitty Litter. Empty one whole bag into the pan. Bury your head in it. Put the other bag on your head.

Tie yourself to the standpipe with the hose. Put the nozzle in your mouth. Turn the water on all the way. You'll never be thirsty again.

Any time is nap time,
especially if there's an
inclined driveway around.
Take your nap at about
6:30 AM. snuggled up
against the rear
wheel of the car.

Find the plastic bags. You'll need one large and one small plus some rubber bands. Get into the large bag. Pull the small one over your head. Fix the bands near the end of each bag. Lie down near your food dish.

Get the jug of bleach, the can of floor wax, and the bottle with the picture of a clogged drain on it. Pour half of each container into the fish pond. Drink the rest. Get into the pool.

If you're one of those cats who are handy with tools, you may choose the cat-door guillotine. Use this Final Exit on Bastille Day.

The electrified flea collar. Chew the ends off an extension cord. Attach the bare wire ends to the metal buckle on your collar. Plug it in. This method also kills fleas.

Part IV
Good Sports

Cats are born athletes.
Why not add the thrill
of competition to your
Final Exit?

The pitching machine at your local amusement center. Set it for 60 mph hardball. Stand on home plate. Your head should be right in the strike zone.

Find the bowling ball.
It's in the hall closet.
Tie the new puppy's leash
to the clothesline. Put
it on. Call the puppy.
He'll be in the yard
underneath you. Grab
the ball and jump.
Just before everything
turns black, drop the ball
... on the puppy.

Live in a single story house? Raid the drawers. Tie together all the bras and panty hose you can find. Try a bungee jump.

The StairStepper.
Eat a dozen fried eggs,
a pound of bacon, a can
of Crisco...drink 10
cups of coffee.
Set the machine on
extra fast for one
hour.

Become the mascot for your local skydiving club. They all have parachutes, but all you need is a cape.

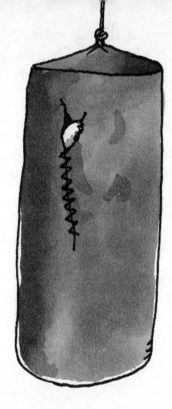

Go to the gym where
the boxers work out. Cut
a slit in the heavy bag.
Climb in. Wait.

Pole vaulting makes for a splashy Final Exit, especially if you can locate a compound of vicious Dobermans.

Are flying saucers for real? They are at the skeet shooting club. Climb aboard one in its launcher. This method is called the flying finish.

Part V
Fairground Exits

A good time for your final exit is when the fair or rodeo or carnival comes to your town. Cats usually get in free.

Notice how the ferris wheel always stops to let people off right when you are at the top? Pretend you think it's broken. Get out of your seat and climb down on the edge of the wheel.

Take your cotton candy with you.

Get on the moving belt in the shooting gallery. Do you think that anyone would shoot at a live target? Probably not.

Bring scissors. Jump onto the balloon man's head and set those balloons free. When the people look like ants, cut the balloons free again. Keep the scissors pointing down.

The bumper cars. See that strange-looking kid with the earring? Sit on the bumper of his car.

Some parks have Killer whales in a tank. They get little fish rewards for doing big tricks. Tie a herring around your neck and jump in. Maybe he'll do a trick for you.

Part VI
Other Methods

The local scene is rich in Final Exit opportunities. Get involved in your community.

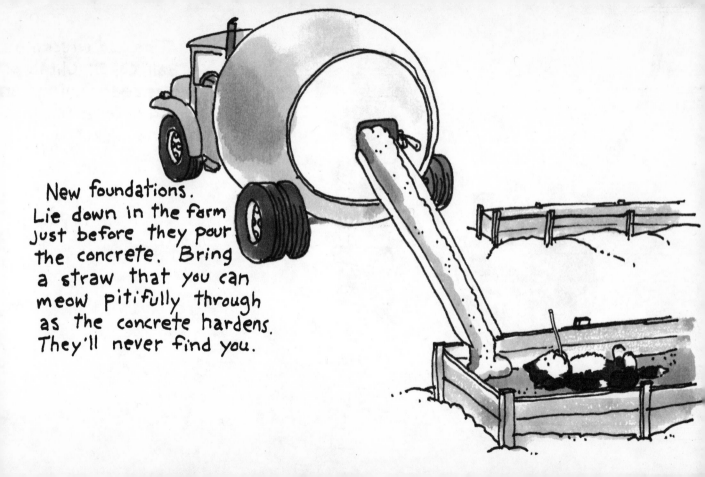

New foundations.
Lie down in the farm
just before they pour
the concrete. Bring
a straw that you can
meow pitifully through
as the concrete hardens.
They'll never find you.

The old wrecking
ball caper. Climb on
between swings an
ride to a smashin
Final Exit.

There must be a
motorcycle in the
neighborhood. Thread
your body through the
spokes of the back
wheel. Grab the
bottom chain. Rest
your chin on the
top chain... wait.

Ever had to travel in the baggage compartment? Never again! Climb into that big round thing hanging off the wing. It's the heater.

Highway cones add a dash of color to your Final Exit. Move one to the other side of the yellow line. Crawl under. Go to sleep. Wait.

Filling potholes is a
community service.
Especially on streets
marked TRUCK ROUTE.

Go to the zoo. Bring some Krazy Glue. Fill an empty peanut shell with it. Sneak through the bars and feed it to the elephant. Laugh at him.

Go to the reptile house.
Climb in with the python.
Wet your tail down so you
look like a big mouse.

Raid the lingerie drawer and the cosmetic bag. Go to a leather bar. Order milk. Spit it in the face of the first guy who makes a remark.

Why not a cruise for your Final Exit? Bring some rope. Sneak aboard. They'll never find you on the anchor.

Find a Pinto. Pry open the trunk. Disconnect the brake lights. Close the trunk. Wait.

You can walk on those
high-tension wires just
like the squirrels do.
Bring a metal pole
for balancing.

Slick down your head and body with hair gel. Sneak into a mink farm. Get in line.

PROCESSING

Look for a great big nest. Kick the babies out. Maybe the mama bird will bring you a nice final treat!

Volunteer for a high-aying industrial testing program.

Locate a hornets' nest. Swing into it and dig all your teeth and claws in. Hold on. Begin your scream when you start your swing.

Notice how the glare of headlights makes you freeze up. Kind of thrilling. Hey! There's lots of headlights over by the highway.

How about a good rat chase before your Final exit? Try the toxic waste dump. No rats? That's strange. Maybe they're hiding under the debris ... or in one of those barrels.

Put a bunch of stamps on a sturdy box. Address it like the one in the picture. Put it out by the mailbox. Crawl in and tape the opening from the inside. Don't bother with a return address.

Part VII
Aftermath

DON'T JUST Leave a note. Leave a multi-page document. Make copies.

Don't settle for a conventional burial or cremation. Make this clear.

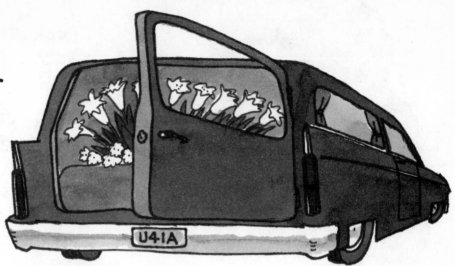

Look through the yellow pages. Find a lawyer who might be in tune with cats. Lawsuits may come about as a result of your Final Exit. Have the lawyer mail any money from these to the author of this book.

Mail copies of the legal
documents to your owners'
church, the ASPCA, and
the *National Enquirer*.
To the lawyer too,
  of course.

No coffin for you!
Insist on a container
with your likeness
carved on it. Your
food dish, catnip mouse,
and some wadded-up
balls of paper should
be in there with you.

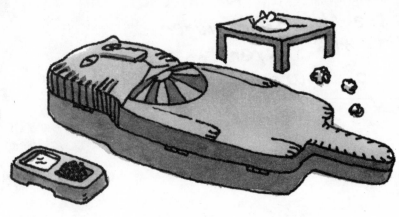

Don't settle for a burial plot. A tomb shaped like a pyramid is best. It must have a cat door in case all that stuff about spirits and afterlife is true.

Stipulate that once every year your owner should bring all your offspring and their offspring to your tomb to pay homage. At this time a sacrifice of the youngest, most attractive member is appropriate.

Grave robbers may be a problem. Remember to include a curse in your documents. If they open your container, feel free to haunt your former owners. Peer in windows and walk around the house at night knocking over lamps and vases.

If they manage to catch you and put you back in the tomb, don't worry. You can pull this off a total of nine times.

Entertainment veteran Michael Viner has produced five feature films, including Columbia Pictures' *Touched by Love*, starring his wife, Deborah Raffin, and winner of the prestigious Christopher Award. His next feature film release will be *Change of Heart*, based on LaVyrle Spencer's *Morning Glory*.

As the president of Dove Audio, Inc., Michael produces best-selling books on cassette. In addition, he has produced and cowritten a number of miniseries, including *The Sands of Time* and *Memories of Midnight*, based on the Sidney Sheldon classics.

He began his writing career as an assistant to political columnist Jack Anderson, reporting on assignment from such remote locations as Hungary, India, and Iran. He has also written the current book *365 Ways You Can Save the Earth*.

Frank Remkiewicz is an author/illustrator of children's books. He has been a staff illustrator for Norcross Greeting. Recent books include the N.Y. *Times* ten best pick *The Last Time I Saw Harris* and *Greedyanna*. His artwork can also be found on the box of an ever-popular brand of animal crackers. He lives in Northern California with his wife and three daughters, all of whom love cats most of the time.